Copyright © 2019 Xiao Yue Shan

All rights reserved.

Cover design by Xiao Yue Shan
Book design by Chelsea Wales - Frontier Poetry

No part of this book may be reproduced in any form or by any electronic or mechanical means including information storage and retrieval systems, without permission in writing from the author. The only exception is by a reviewer, who may quote short excerpts in a review.

Xiao Yue Shan
Visit my website at www.shellyshan.com

Published in the United States of America by Frontier Poetry
www.frontierpoetry.com

PRAISE FOR SHAN'S POETRY

"Xiao Yue Shan's poems are both alight and firmly buried into the earth at the same time. What a wonderful discovery of Shan's poems. In a poem, "the worth of a woman's life in China," Shan writes: "in china they say a man is like a mountain/and a woman is like a river. it is because we spread/to fill empty spaces." Shan's poems both create spaces we didn't know existed and spread to fill them with new words and combinations of words. Definitely a poet to watch!" — Victoria Chang, Guggenheim Fellow & author of *Barbie Chang*

"I'm bonkers for these poems. Be still my heart. The love of this world, its inhabitants painted with all palettes from dusky to florescent to bloody, infuses every line in this volume. Like many of 'us' today, I am drowning in books. This book made me want to drown right in its pages. I'll be reading it on repeat." — Jordan A. Y. Smith, Editor-in-Chief of *Tokyo Poetry Journal*

"Creation myth does not do justice to the ambition of Xiao Yue Shan's poems which, by straddling the mythical-poetic and the historical, transform both into a vision that is completely the poet's own. Shan's lines have the effect of being simultaneously heavy and effortless—a quality that rhymes beautifully with her speaker's prevailing attitude of critical fascination with the world. From the injustices of history to the injustices of the present, from the joys of childhood to the wisdom of adulthood, Shan's poems bring us into intimate engagement with her inner world" — Simon Shieh, Editor-in-Chief of *Spittoon Literary Magazine*

HOW OFTEN I HAVE CHOSEN LOVE

FOR MY MOTHER, 张冠伟
FOR MY FATHER, 单连泉

when I was four years old my parents took me to tiananmen square

1.

in the train car from dongying
to beijing, the light, 3am humming, sleeps
in strange directions. different weights

of yellow. I close my eyes,
dizzy. mama's warm hand greying exhale
against my forehead, the world

escapes by in the window, like fleeing.
I didn't realize it was we
who were running, and everything else

was still. it takes time
to figure out different kinds
of quiet. like how colours come

to belong to their names, and if blue ever
gets bluer. there are boiled chestnuts
in mama's coat, and she cracks them for me

one by one until
we arrive at tiananmen
in time for dawn. the sun

looks as if it was put
hastily in the sky. hesitant despite having risen
the same way for ever. a flag is raised

into it, as if this is the thing
that makes and unmakes
the day.

2.

feed the dead raw silk and organza.
feed them gold-plated sunflower
seeds in water-chipped ming bowls,
holy basil, wild ginger. feed them white
buns with hearts of brown
sugar, spooned porridge under pink
cotton quilts in bouts of childhood
fever. feed them freshwater pearls.
they were loved. they were the most
loved. in a garden plant 200 or 1000
orchids, shoot the bulbs into the
ground. pile gunpowder over them.
hope they will still grow stalks of
colour. feed the dead soft plums
and seawater. give them something
to bite on, before you begin to
remember.

3.

mama knit stories. a woman who filled
the ocean with milkstones,
a girl and a rabbit and a peach tree

on the moon. stories steeled in centuries
that sang our blood
a chinese blood. myths barefoot to the strain

of erhu strings. a sky boiling
under nine suns, crossing seas
upon a sword— stories

we do not negotiate
as we do facts
about how many died

and where. and when. and men packed
like tindersticks, some
light between them. I watched

mama's shoulders downward
in front of an oil portrait, hung over a fiery shade
of carmine that everyone knows

means lucky.
I'm in a green dress.
papa takes my photo, standing

in a thrill of poppy and chrysanthemum,
under the painting of a man who looks
like my grandfather.

4.

let me walk down the paper-white roads of chengdu one more time. let me
green my arm in the waters of songhua river, glance over my
grandmother's table. let me watch the steam weeping from windows
down shangde avenue. let me do it without bravery.

let me swim in the yangtze. let me
touch the softening cheeks of my mother. let me put my daughter's
shoes on for her. give me time to figure out how to be more
than water. let me see my home town through the smoke
of my uncle's cigarette. let me please see november. let this day pass
without my having done anything to end it.

5.

it is a red light that sounds through the flag
and I am experiencing, in a little life,
the closest thing yet

to prayer. the palm,
the white glove,
the breast, fine

and whole. no one admits june fourth
through the gates, so we all stand around flowers
and little girls and we say;

pretty. remember our names do not have long to live
either. we are lucky if they even
grow old with us. oh, and, the day is the thing

that gets blue
and bluer. someone had a dream that heaven
could be a modifier for earthly

peace, then men died, and the next morning
we woke up complicit. liars
when our feet

touched the land.
with noonshine sounding copper
on my wrists, I watched papa's spine iron

with pride. his china, the spring front ancient
and careful, our breathing
not filled with ghosts, but

mulberries. chang-an jie is ripe and glossed
with bodies, smoking and laughing and beginning
things. I looked both ways and couldn't see

the end of it.

and hong kong in 2001 was always this shade of light blue

papa was a communist / mama worked in a factory
making parts for / airplanes
it wasn't quite proper / for girls to stay out all day
coming home with black oil / on the pales of fine necks
but I guess we / needed the money
the kitchen at night / shined of cigarette smoke
and bare hot-july chests / men swilling warm beer
yellow slick skin / steamed chestnut shells
grease throat laughter / glass spilling laughter
white-blue hong kong dusk / peppering our mouths
through the open / window
the balcony brimmed / with pots of laundry water
stalks of lucky bamboo / red-gold ribbon curls
it was / too loud to sleep
so I curled on / papa's knee
half naked / among the sunflower seeds
overflowing ashtrays / black sesame cakes
mama putting on lipstick / over the steaming stove
occasionally threatening / to call someone's wife
and the hungry skyline / no longer fit
into the neon basin / of shing min river
around the table / red cheeks red palms
they were taxi drivers / low-level beaucrats
shined woks / pulled rickshaws
loved their country / just enough
papa had skinny arms / skimpy black moustache
mama wore hoop earrings / a filthy mouth
sometimes I wish we / never left china
with 50000 yuan / a single suitcase
that they kept laughing / chain-smoking
popping caps / off green tsingtao bottles
doing bad impressions / of their bosses
some teresa teng song / swaying the hot air
a smell of smoked duck / steamed sweet potato
in that 400 square foot / one bedroom apartment
where no one ever got / to finish a sentence

the girls of harbin
for my mother, zhang guanwei

they call them northern lilacs, winter beauties. they say coral-
hawberry cheeks in nomadic january, that between the baroque quarters
of songhua river you can see the small hem of a gold-brocade cashmere
kissing the ice-crushed curb. they say in harbin, you can watch
girls just walk, forever. that she sweeps through the city
and the streets make music against her body. in heilongjiang, the days
are so short for so long, but the light loves the skin it lands on—
seemingly staying for awhile, breathlessly frosting,
hinting of water, before washing itself away. they say the further north
the further you are from heaven. and maybe that's why the girls here
are milk-bathed, long-necked, laughing, shaking out their hair
from glazed-shell pins, looking at you that way. no matter where
they are, they're thirsty for a winter that blurs the edges of when
their shoulders meet the air, pale as horizon. they say when russia came
with its railroads and cathedrals and black bread, it was
girls with whom they drank vodka from porcelain bowls, tearing
red sausage teeth-first from coal-charred steel, girls with eyes
and lips satin as ricepaper, girls measured with peaches,
girls daughters of refugees and criminals and girls who knew
the needlepoint of new snow against raw fingertips, combing through
the land, knitted with ice like lacework, for something, oh, anything
to eat. it is because the winter-earth has been thawed by blood, here,
that they say you will never hurt a girl from harbin. that she wears honey
on her breath but doesn't talk sweet. that she'll break a window
before she opens a door. that she eats ice cream in the dead of december,
licking a black sesame drip from a bare wrist. girls in harbin know to never
complain about the cold. they press it to their chests as a bouquet
of bluebells. or a blade under the sleeve. and through shuangcheng
to yilan you don't get tired of watching girls walk. the winter chrysalis
shedding in mid-may turns the day orange, dripping so, and
you'll see them in their thigh-skimming skirts, lips just-bitten red,
throwing a sudden black braid over the shoulder, tossing easy
a wind that always blows north-ward, disrupting the timid spring day
like a wild peony bursting, breaking the bud with one flick of a silken skirt.

ornithomancy

on peace boulevard some engine thunder sends
stray pavement tumbling, and in the black
dust of travel an ear is put to the ground to hear
the idiolect of footpaths, mineral-old, still
somehow speaking. language pulling knots in
the veins of the city. traffic serving its metronomic,
hypnotic purpose. beijing whose cartography
was modelled after the angelic. from gem-windows
thriving skyward, the dimmed land still gathers up
breath and smoke all in some apparition,
a city in gauze looking almost like heaven. a city
in bandages amidst its own demolition. no one
will ever again say that it's just like we never left.
what's left? camphor and paper houses.
the orange light is purple and grey and too-blue.

between the slender courtyard walls it seems
everything is counting on all this being kept
just between us. a carved sparrow trying to fly from
the pear-wood frame before its contractual, imminent
expropriation. a city clerk marries his pen
to the page and two days later mingshan houjie
is smoke and knee-deep in a red rage, ochre
brick broken from walls once laced through with
the scripture of thin broths, secrets, ceremony.
the children born on this ground were always
ancient. their stunning bodies calling backward,
backward, a lineage of soil and clay. here we
buried milk names. here we lit golden bells.
and as the razing rhythms on we lock the doors
that no longer serve their purpose of protecting.
at our feet shatters a sparrow's wings, wide
amidst chipped sprays of chrysanthemum,
toothless eaves, pale tiles scattered like petals.

willingly into the muting blue

all the while down minsheng road the cars curl around one another, almost kissing. in the dark looking enough like bodies that it was easy to forget they had people inside of them.

smog glared against the sky. grey on grey.

somebody said this wasn't ordinary traffic. somebody had a hot dinner waiting back at home.

eight pm sees teenagers just out of class. angels against glory-white doorways. the convenience store named after the moon. hand-warmed bottles of too-sweet tea. pink cream pastry, bare forearms and cheeks blue and perfect in the cellophane light.

wives, holding plastic flowers, spilling over the street-corner. someone invents the tangerine peony.

in the middle of the qizheng courtyard a tall bust of venus, piano-white. shadows doing work hands cannot. no one knows who built her or why one shoulder slopes, our marbled swan in foreign river-water. no one lives in the qizheng buildings, not for a long time.

pride, maybe. or guilt from not coming home more often.

goldfish tied to hooks on the pavilion we're still laughing.

streets of oyster-shell pattern.

the tallest gravestones in the huang shan cemetery are still the ones for the russians. mandarin prayers for slavic names. stalks of closed tulips. tissue-paper aster, carefully purple, frosting over.

it is said that the ghosts of the occupiers feel just as at home as the ghosts of the occupied.

woman selling hawberries in syrup outside the old synagogue. between her and the arched doorway a pure, white space.

beer and warm vodka. beer and warm vodka. she sits at the table in her high collar opening bottles all night. beer and warm vodka. she drinks when they tell her to drink. she smiles her small, close-lipped smile.

the sound of water being poured into a hot wok is so familiar it reminds everyone of their mothers.

cars parked on sidewalks. cars the meeting place for furtive trades. cars driven in walnut trees.

back end of a truck filled with green-stained wooden slats. front end of the truck nowhere to be found.

the gift of grapefruit on a tuesday. the shop just got them in. how do you eat this she asks, tapping the rippled skin with a fingernail.

the thing about uninhabitable places is that you have to wonder who lives there.

don't fall asleep in the car. your spirit won't know the way back home.

easy to tell who was raised right by the way they pick out fruit. heaviest ones are juiciest. thinly pressing the bursting skin of a nectarine. knuckles knocked against watermelon rinds.

her needle digs tiny tunnels along the seam, the thread following like river-water.

cold that the air freezes clean. nothing leaves a trace, save for the astonished breath turning into snow.

in the window: silk, dried plums, cutting board, wool socks.

they said that all the pretty girls were cabaret hostesses, and all the ugly ones were dentists.

a man reads the paper and shells beef into white buns, selling them for eight yuan through a half-cracked door. glass impressioned with grime. letters in red and less red.

in winter harbin is a diamond. city somehow orienting itself around its prisms.

she's in bed wearing a yellow nightgown. light from other apartments sheening colour on her still face. her little hand on top of the crochet pillowcase.

we are still inheriting linens from our great-grandmothers.

tomorrow is the sun and moon nestled next to one another. then the sky.

day red day blue day.

the nation of aphasia

when a writer goes missing in china
we take the red and gold paper emblems
that display the character for luck
off of our doors and paste them
over our mouths. and we go back to
the old books to learn again
what we've learned for millennia,
that you can command armies or
recompose history or traverse
from xian to changsha to mount lu
or buy a dozen eggs and none of it
will mean that your life is a promise
your country makes to you.
hong kong is a dewdrop glittering
in mid-january. we close our eyes
to take its temperature, trying to find
just the right word. the rain
only a sweet-tasting silhouette against
the gleaming skyline. late-day light
spreads a white sheet over the windows
and no one can see in. no one can see out.
still, no one ever thinks this is the day
someone will knock on the door
asking you to identify your husband
by his handwriting. how is it that
we have made a culture out of
paying a heavy price. wearing out stones
with water. chasing the sun across
the eastern front with our poems
closing in behind us like lost birds.
the gardens we do not tend. the paper
boats we do not try in the yangtze.
imagine your life is the thing
that is trapped on the tip of your tongue,
the word that is almost realized,
but you can't quite think of.

ideogram of morning

over rooftops written
        timidly into the city like
                fiction, we waited

for the day
        thickly blue
                between our teeth

pristine cotton light
        unpacking flora
                onto our limbs

chiaroscuro
        of cold juniper
                silvering wisteria

trying to start
        with our bodies
                a dialogue about colour

we bore witness
        to our own
                creation myth

and the red
        was in exactly
                the right place

you were
        a perfect compromise
                a truce on the white concrete

like someone
        all of a sudden
                thought

to build into a window
        what the light looks like
                as it is passing through

explain to me fate as if I were a child

how do things come up to be next
to one another. streets with no names
pressed poorly upon mountains, molasses
twilight holding the day, hip
pushed to hip during rush hour,
and old photographs leaving yellow oil
upon the new. the city-bound flocking
above the river-water, the benevolent
laying her hands on the unforgivable,
the living light that eagerly tenderizes
the dying one. how does a child
meet the future just so,
how do sprouts meet their flowers,
how do various evenings meet in the kitchen
over broths and breads. how many pairs
of hands carried fruit to this bowl.
what rhythm of music led some eyes
from here, to a place a little more
dangerous. how did we come to be with
one another, here as if enchanted, with
no more reason than two grains of sand,
and no less intoxication than two winds,
infuriated by the distance
they've both had to come.

梦

I lay my head down on a pillow pilled
with characters, yellow tracks and traces
of the name I was given. I sleep
on chinese every night. I speak
dialects inside my head, words strange and
pelagic. words harnessed to a shore. language
that asks for directions back to the main street,
for a second helping, for a mother. there is a child
whose head fits where mine does, upon
cotton worn to silk by years and years
of sleep. I do not know how to speak chinese
that does not belong to the child. I know how
to ask for milk but not scissors. I know how to ask
to be held but not to explain why. I bite down
hard on a word. black sesame word, warm tofu word,
morning words. in the mid-minute above waking
I remember every moment of a dream,
before forgetting.

when you plant a seed in vietnam it grows and grows

the mekong seems like the edge of the world
but it can't be. that would mean we came

                      from somewhere,

but behind there's nothing but green.
moon, moths, the oily throats of wild banana trees

                      all green.

the woman rows the boat and she is green, her skin
takes root. this water, thick and dark as the mouths

                      of doves,

seems home to even far away places. a man dips his feet
into it, sways. holds. he is drinking. light freezes

                      and does not touch.

palm fronds and straw-stems and blue tarps
float and then are swallowed. here the earth

                      takes from us.

everything we relinquish and abandon
she receives and weighs in her hand, forces it

                      to bear fruit.

fruit that is sweet to the point of seeming
mysterious. here our bodies are salt and

                      the light licks at us

as if we were a wound she wanted to heal.
here one only has to open a mouth to be relieved

                      of thirst.

the whole air is here. whole days of clouds.
we fall sleep in sweat and smoke, safe knowing

                      we will wake up green.

search by no light

by   the antibesian waters
of tokyo   bay
I   search   my body
   by   no   light

learning   and naming
what I alone   can touch
leather   pearl
   paper   silver

where   and how
within me contains
artillery
   who put it there   why

the moon   admitted
courting   river birches
light   does not blanch
   hand prints water stains

upon   the skin
past   touches   lie
powdered
   sifted   and   merging

the secret taste
the   bullet   rising
my creation myth
   has   no tale of falling

easier if we cried

sitting across from one another with cigarettes we keep forgetting, san francisco hanging like sheets to be kicked away in the middle of the night. I can tell by how beautiful you are becoming that something different will be said. careful to salt the words before you let them leave. july daze was gauzed around our shoulders, heat that alighted wildflowers, that convinced the sweet out of the wine. you are so thin I would believe someone's rib was used to make you, all deep breaths and clicks of your bad wrist. the bare leaf of your upper back, you're sitting so still but your body looks like

it remembers falling. you say, and then I woke up and this guy I've never seen before was having sex with me. our stupid, heavy language. this wooden, through language that makes a fist out of your beautiful mouth. words naked by light, green-olive bitter, soaked with evening. we always knew we weren't new things. you would point at my collarbone and say, this hollow here, showing me the places love would discover. slights that act as stopping-places for sandy water, jasmine-smell, lips that could not be redder. you say when the right person touches you it feels like grasses growing up between cobblestones, and then you woke up and this guy you've never seen before was- that sounds like rape, I say, too quickly. I don't want to think about it that way. you said. the small linen of your skin, knitted with blush. fingers stiffened in the shape of a pistol. the car that forgot you were in the trunk when it dove into the river. I'm always putting out my hand to find ashtrays

that I didn't know were there. if you never say never, you can't say nevermind. I don't want this to be one of those things where I reach out to take your hand and discover that they are the same size. you are so small, on the other side of the table. candlelight sculpted a mirror of you in the glass, smoothing down the corners. you, softer. I want to not be scared that you would be scared if I touched you. it's for selfish reasons. I don't know how to fix fruit broken with bruised, full bites. peach flesh and shrapnel on your chair. I can't think about it that way, you said, so, so, beautifully. the perfect note of your skin to punctuate the sentence of you and I sitting there. it was july in san francisco. I was holding the word rape in front of your mouth like a knife. all this intention we sacrifice to the open air. I want to pick up the telephone of your mouth and use it to call backwards, ask to speak to you then, just one more time. the silence before you say hello,

on loop. that hollow there.

inheritance

my mother says about hong kong:
that wasn't your life. that was my life.
she meant the chicken boiling with anise
on the stove and the rouge pinking the edge
of the wooden spoon. the broth she raised to
her mouth to taste. she meant I couldn't taste.
too young. she put cotton over my mouth
when we went outside. air softened. it was
her life. all skins of oranges left outside
to dry and the anthemic thunder— this
is not the life I want for my child.
that was her life. I run into hong kong
on the street in the summertime. I say
I got off the plane and came right to see you.
she wears orange. rouge. my mother's face.
upon her so few places to lie. we sit in a cafe
in sheung wan with pink cups eating
bean cakes, and later I call my mother to say
I found our old apartment building.
that I had walked up the blue stairs
and laid my hand on the door.
hong kong a neon neckline, long hair glittering
with ship-lights, crystal balls, storm velvets.
it's her life, yet I had come, and grown
my hair, and happened upon the eastern sun
like a moon. a life pearled into stories
served on porcelain into the mouth
of a hungry child.

the diaspora roommate

coming in from doorways
opposite into a room
that seemed to face whichever way
the sun was coming in, all of the time.
you were hanging clothes with your shoes on
and the room was pendulous
with your testaments—
your furniture. your pictures
and a quilt draped on the bed
made by your grandmother.
when did you get here, I asked.
a little while before you did, you said.
and we stood for awhile unsure
pebbling our individual scripts
with our few common words.
can I sit there, I pointed
to the velvet-looking window seat.
*actually, that's a family heirloom
but you can sit here*, you pulled up
a wooden chair. I smiled. you did too.
I pulled green dates and candied
hawthorns from my pocket
and we shared them. I felt precious
to be with you, when you told me stories
about here. the room was warm
and water white from the tap was cold
and good. you asked me, *why did you
come?* and I said, *I heard good things
about this place*. you liked that. you nodded
with pride. we slept side by side
that night. you on your bed and I
on my coat spread out on the floor.
I didn't have very much. you understood.
I knew that you were here first. you agreed.
but when the patterns of this world
began to show upon my skin
I felt as if I were home. you didn't disagree.
after awhile I seeded some small pots
with anise and papered the drawers
pink and yellow. at night you asked me questions
and I answered them. *my father's farm.
chives and cabbages. the mountains.
some places especially enchanted*

on the edge of october.
you let your hand fall
and touched the floor, as if
testing the temperature. I lit sticks of incense
stuck into oranges and told stories
infinite as the evening. you played records
that did sound exactly like blue.
sometimes I called home.
sometimes we shared cigarettes.
sometimes we spared one another
the little indignities of writing names
on bags of apples. sometimes we didn't.
we varied in shape and left trails
of different colours as we moved
here and forth, across the room.
I loved you from certain angles—
your different astrology, newspapers,
and you loved the things I gave
without knowing. the sweet taste of salt
and sheets of wild silk, thin as sprouts,
some things we never managed
to teach one another. the feeling of hot oil.
prayers. the xi of my name.
you soundlessly replaced certain
things of mine. a word here.
a taste, a colour elsewhere. and when
it became cold I sometimes pulled
your grandmother's quilt from your bed
and wrapped myself deep within it.
I did not feel guilty to know what
was yours, and what was mine. we lived
without consciousness. we were not careless
though from beyond the window it may
have seemed so. we did not have
a mutual language by which to explain
why. the small room and its white
concrete walls unfolded
in various blooms. single light.
multitudinous voices. our respective
breathing revolving.
you, who was here first.
and I, who was here anyway.

in which we have never returned from our wars

when waiting becomes something   to measure
    eternity   with
and because time   is without quantity
it is able to detain   a whole country in
    dark   oaken   stasis
violence   was shared equal   between the land
and the bodies   of our youth
    during   the winter   of 1969
spaces gouged   deep within them
    as if something   green
may one day   grow there

eventually all things   come to   rest
on the horizon   even our children
    the stiff fields of maize   and sorghum
continued to be tended   for new seed
even as the mothers   on their knees
within them   paused   again and again
    disbelieving   the   barren   days
    unfolding   letters
from their sons   who were somewhere
in xinjiang   or siberia
and having to find   one of the three men
left in the village   who could read

    november bleeding   into february
my father answered   a knock at the door
    every   couple   of weeks
receiving mail from   his classmates
    who had not   been able
to afford gloves   in their school days
he read passages   aloud   to waiting parents
it's just   *a little cold*   *not so bad*
sometimes   he received   lightbulbs
in brown paper   still warm   as thanks

         my father   the patriot   believed
            in the greatness   of country
      and the men   willing to die   many
         ordinary deaths—   by ice   by starvation
                       for   it
                 still   the bodies
         deified by frost   seemed shameful
                like all   things done
            where our mothers   cannot see

               strange   to think
      that a nation can build itself up   and wide
            and grey   without days ever seeming
      to have gone by   men blackened by snow and
      living on paper   with them standing
      so still like this   hands open like this

the worth of a woman's life in china

never looking backward. never calling out
their names. your accusers. your torturers.
picking up the long-soft fruits of a gone summer,
never straying too close to the water.
in china they say a man is like a mountain
and a woman is like a river. it is because we spread
to fill empty spaces. because we allow for
greenness. it is because they drink
freely from us. because they carve routes
upon us. because when our lifeless bodies are swept
into the delta it can be said that we are simply
returning. they may then rinse the blood
from their hands with our hems. perhaps
it is that we slowly darken with their dirt,
their sand, their spit, their sweat,
their urine. in the dim throb of moonlight
a thousand chinese daughters melt into
the fertile soil. millet will be grown there. oilseed,
cotton. and in the speed by which crops of autumn
come a thousand more girls will be bowed,
mouth-first, into the land. to be seeded,
to be plough. it cannot be seen from above, but only
from looking backward. yet when standing upon
an edge one does not glance behind,
but only beyond. so it is that these daughters
continue to become wives, continue to become
mothers. so it is that the good women
have survived! upon the paths crawled deep
by slender forearms, by black plaits shorn close
to the skull. upon the ground cultivated by
a monthly blood, good women have walked. those who
take no notice of their scars, for they no longer
hurt. truly we have come far. truly we have come here.
here the daughters of this splendid, instant metropolis
are dwelled and glittering into hotel windows,
oscillating rings of bluish light, jacquard gowns
and jewels upon the toes of high-heeled shoes.

their soft bodies threaded in and out
of bedroom doorways and rimmed with pastel
laces. yet baited by the crystalline
frame the silken bed is beaten into a hook
upon which the act of using is synonymous with the act
of making love. yes, the glass candelabras. yes,
the swollen green rings of jade. yes, the millennial
shade of lipstick! yes, the lozenges made from pearl-dust!
they are escorted from girlhood in the blaze
of a pinking glory! nothing like the university students
of the revolution who plucked slivers of bamboo
from the deeps of their thighs. nothing like the childless
mothers of northern earthquakes. nothing like porridge
and boiled cabbage every night. violence
has slipped into richer clothing. it has been cured
from stone into diamond. yes, it can no longer be said
that we are worthless, for we can be weighed,
wrapped. we can be sold. we can be purchased.
at train stations and fruit stands and fragrant department
stores, and of course, what can be bought can also
be stolen. they still pull us into gutters.
pass us off to fellow soldiers. they have used the mouths
of bottles and the branches of firs. they still do, though there are
new, more intricate ways to destroy. new concrete steps
stitched crooked to the side of the same cascade, same river.
same wreckage, same water. where have we travelled
in never looking backward. never naming
our devourers. our inflictors. what is the worth
of a woman's life in china. I'll tell you. it is the life
of every man who has spit into her water.

how often I have chosen love

how often I have chosen love
in the chestnut of november
when the night cracks open and is yellow
the dusk lifts the city up towards mid-air
how it stays there
pendulating and trembling
grasped in the palm-sized wind

daily how I have chosen the lemon tree
hanging over the slatted rooftop
and tatami shade
copper-colour, time-stoned
every shape of the moon having made
itself upon it
bearing fruit
such heavy living fruit
to be picked by no one

how every rained-in morning
spoke itself in unison
just as I have chosen to meet it
and all the distance was electric
pretty girls standing paled
roman windows spun with wire
along the circle paths of daikanyama
river pebbles

how I have chosen to love a city
that takes from other cities
the whole of tokyo a lockbox
overflown with photos of flowers
passing the bike rack by nakameguro station
upon which miki had brushed her hair
and taught me dirty words in japanese
few leaves clinging
I imagined I heard the sound green made
threading the cherry trees

how often I have chosen the sumida
and the sight from the middle
standing on the red bridge looking
at the blue bridge
as a man pours half a bottle of whiskey
into the river and it whirled
inward like a handprint

should I mention the fingernail moon

how I had once boarded a train to ibaraki
and peeled mandarin oranges
until citrus drowned the stale air
I watched heels dig perfect circles
into the snow and seedlings shot up
from where precisely they had stood
it was easy to imagine
what could be watercolour
a painted moment otherwise gone
saved for later

names of people do not come as easily
as the names of rivers
at the photographic museum I saw
a flock of birds all rise at once
save for one who nailed
a piece of the ground underneath him

how often we sat by the heating lamp
smoking our different cigarettes
as their tails drew non-figures upward
we read them as symbols
you did not look at me at first and then
you looked at me
my hand was painted into the dim
in yanaka the trees grew into houses
and we did not spend too much time thinking
about who lived here before

how clouds turned into gold once
they touched the ground in shinjuku
how lightbulbs shed their cloud-glow
upon those who kissed under them

ikegami: in the mute plum garden
combed through whitely
by generations of hands
starlight is vivified when reflected
off the skin of a plum

how I had walked
on music shed by passersby careless
leaving strings of words dangling
handed to me adjacently
from both sides
even sometimes laughter
even sometimes ginger flowers
passed over and I took them

the acquiescing light tied around
wild-pink buildings
by some hand wishing
I take it a sign of my good youth
that I am still enraptured by sunsets

how I was taught the right way to pray
with a ten yen coin
by someone who loved me
up an uncountable number of stairs
the jagged papers spun
as though the forces of our shadows
inhumanly elongated
ruffled the hems of a spiritdom
there were three anonymous flowers
growing from the stone

how often fresh figs were cracked
against the concrete linings in toyama-koen
capsuled in droplets of lilac sun
their sweet smell

how often I have chosen love
upon this ground every block charted
by prodigal feet, by unnamed rulers
in the onset of winter a cartography emerges
a heart startles heavy
traffic blindly intersecting
in tokyo where there is no patience
after having chosen

ACKNOWLEDGEMENTS

Thank you to these publications, in which the following poems originally appeared:

Redivider Journal:
"the nation of aphasia"
"the girls of harbin"

Grain Magazine:
"and hong kong in 2001 was always this shade of light blue"

The Asian American Writers' Workshop:
"ornithomancy"
"梦"

The Briar Cliff Review:
"the worth of a woman's life in china"

Aesthetica Creative Writing Annual 2019:
"easier if we cried"

www.ingramcontent.com/pod-product-compliance
Lightning Source LLC
Chambersburg PA
CBHW051959290426
44110CB00015B/2312